Contents

EDUCATIONAL BOARD: Monique Datta, EdD, Asst. Professor, Rossier School of Education, USC; Karyn Saxon, PhD, Elementary Curriculum Coordinator, Wayland, MA; Francie Alexander, Chief Academic Officer, Scholastic Inc.

Distributed in the UK by Scholastic UK Ltd, Westfield Road, Southam, Warwickshire, England CV47 0RA

ISBN 978 1407 13839 8
12 11 10 9 8 7 6 5 4 3 2 1   13 14 15 16 17 18/0
Printed in the USA 40
First published 2013

Scholastic is constantly working to lessen the environmental impact of our manufacturing processes. To view our industry-leading paper procurement policy, visit www.scholastic.com/paperpolicy.

Titanic sinks!

Titanic tilted down into the water. All its lights went out. Terrified people clung to the sides of the ship. With a huge noise, *Titanic* split in two and sank. The screams of 1,500 people filled the freezing air. Far away, survivors in lifeboats held hands as they watched and listened in horror. One of them was Eva Hart. She knew that her father was in the icy water.

Young eyewitness

Eva Hart, aged seven, sailed on *Titanic* with her parents. Later, she wrote about what she had seen.

SOS

I have lived and relived the dying moments of the *Titanic* many times since I sat cold and miserable, crying for my father, in that small lifeboat bobbing about on the icy waters of the Atlantic.

Eva Hart saw the

2,223 passengers and crew member

This was the scene in the early morning of Monday, 15 April 1912. *Titanic*, the ship that everyone said was unsinkable, had hit an iceberg. It filled with water and sank within hours. *Titanic* is the most famous shipwreck in history.

...ailed on *Titanic*. Only 706 survived the sinking.

The ultimate ship

Titanic was the world's latest wonder. It was the biggest, most luxurious ship on the seas. *Titanic* was built in Belfast, Ireland, by a team of 15,000 men. Inside, it looked like a palace. First-class passengers could eat in smart cafés or swim in the pool. Second-class bedrooms were very comfortable. Third-class passengers had a room for music and dancing. Most homes did not have electricity, but *Titanic* was lit by 10,000 lightbulbs.

1 captain,
Edward John Smith

898 crew members

This is the hull of *Titanic*'s sister ship. *Titanic* was slightly bigger.

Titanic by the numbers

About 3 million rivets held the ship together.

Titanic had 1,200 portholes.

The ship was 11 storeys tall and 269 metres (882.8 ft.) long.

e most
pensive ticket
st about £78,300
today's money.

$

To feed the passengers
and crew, *Titanic* carried:

40,000
eggs

1,000 loaves
of bread

36,000
apples

Titanic was as luxurious as a good hotel. It also had the latest safety features. People thought that it was unsinkable. It had special areas that were supposed to be watertight. Even if the ship was damaged, it would stay afloat. People could be rowed to safety in lifeboats.

The lifeboats were stored on the top deck. They were lowered on ropes from steel arms..

THINK ABOUT IT **If you were on board**

Titanic was ready to sail from England to the United States on 10 April 1912. The world was watching the "ship of dreams".

SAFETY FEATURES

Radio

Titanic had the latest radio equipment. This could be used to call for help if needed.

Radio headset

Each red area was watertight.

Watertight sections

The hull, or bottom frame, was split into 16 watertight areas.

Lots of lifeboats

Titanic had more lifeboats than were needed under the law. The 20 lifeboats could carry 1,178 people. This was half the number on board.

On board *Titanic*

All kinds of people sailed on *Titanic*. The very rich travelled in first class. Among them was Margaret Brown, an American returning from a holiday in France. Passengers in second class might be teachers or businessmen like

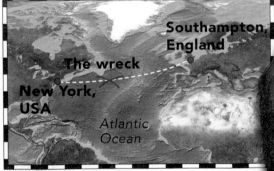

Southampton, England

The wreck

New York, USA

Atlantic Ocean

Titanic's route

Titanic was set to sail more than 4,800 kilometres (3,000 miles) across the ocean.

SOS

Between 1901 and 1910, 8.8 million

First class:
Margaret Brown

Second class:
the Hart family

Third class:
the Goodwin family

Eva Hart's father. The Goodwins and their children were travelling in third class. Like many third-class passengers, they were leaving Europe to find a better life in the United States.

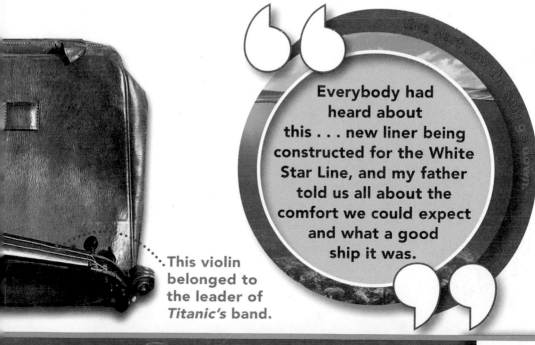

Eva Hart saw the ship go down.

> Everybody had heard about this . . . new liner being constructed for the White Star Line, and my father told us all about the comfort we could expect and what a good ship it was.

This violin belonged to the leader of *Titanic's* band.

The passengers explored *Titanic*'s many rooms. These fitted like jigsaw pieces around big spaces such as the grand staircase, the dining rooms, and the swimming pool. The chart room was at the top of the ship. Inside, officers worked out where the ship was and how far it had travelled.

In the depths of the ship, stokers sweated all day and all night, shovelling coal into boilers.

Titanic cross-section

Chart room

Swimming pool

THINK ABOUT IT **Why were third-clas**

Grand staircase

First-class deck

B Deck: First-class café

F Deck: Third-class dining room

Boilers

Life on *Titanic* was thrilling for every class of passenger. There was something for everyone in the family. Frederic and Daisy Spedden were travelling in first class with their son, Douglas, aged six. Maybe their day looked something like this.

Frederic swam in the pool. He joined his family for breakfast. Then he and Douglas played with a spinning top on the first-class deck.

Children were allowed in the gym between 1 PM and 3 PM. Douglas rode the bicycle and the electric camel. Then he played

First-class passengers could use *Titanic*'s gym

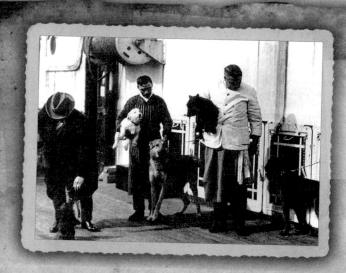

Titanic had a kennel for passengers' dogs.

with the dogs on board when the staff brought them out from their kennels.

The family took an evening promenade before Douglas went to bed. Frederic played cards until lights-out.

NEW WORD

Taking a **promenade** (prah-muh-NAHD), or stroll, was a popular activity on *Titanic*.

SAY IT OUT LOUD

Passengers took promenades before dinner.

Iceberg right ahead

Icebergs are mountains of ice that float in the sea. They did not often float into the route that *Titanic* was following. But there was ice on Sunday, 14 April. Nearby ships sent ice warnings to *Titanic*. Some ships stopped because of the danger, but Captain Smith sailed on into the night at high speed. He was sure that his lookouts would spot any trouble and that *Titanic* was a safe ship.

But it is hard to see an iceberg in a dark, calm sea. When one appeared just ahead, *Titanic* swerved but could not avoid it. The iceberg scraped along the side of the ship. Five watertight areas started to flood.

TIMELINE 14 APRIL 1912

14 April, 9:12 AM
Titanic received the first of many ice warnings.

14 April, 10:00 AM
Lifeboat practice was cancelled. No one knows why.

14 April, 7:00 PM
Titanic sailed at its fastest speed so far.

14 April, 10:00 PM
New lookouts went on duty. Their binoculars were lost.

14 April, 11:07 PM
The last warning wasn't passed on to Captain Smith.

14 April, 11:40 PM
A lookout rang a bell and yelled, "Iceberg right ahead."

14 April, 11:40 PM
Titanic scraped against the iceberg.

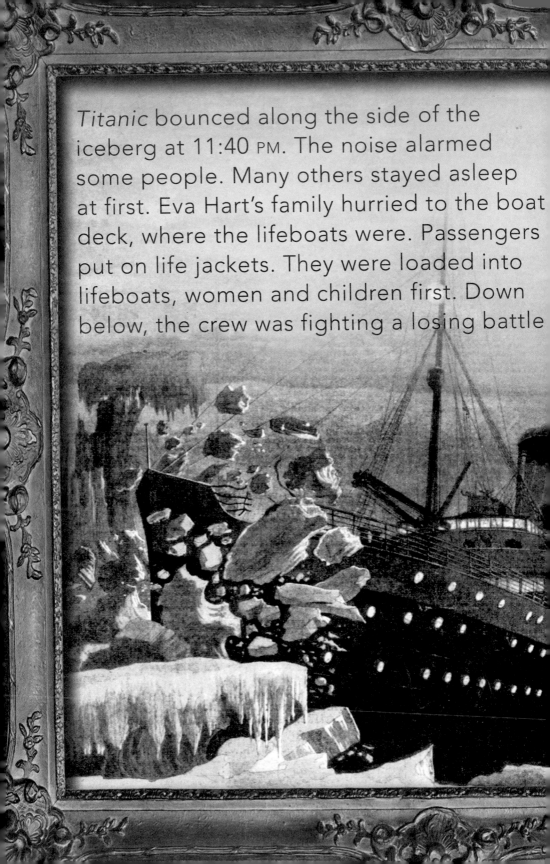

Titanic bounced along the side of the iceberg at 11:40 PM. The noise alarmed some people. Many others stayed asleep at first. Eva Hart's family hurried to the boat deck, where the lifeboats were. Passengers put on life jackets. They were loaded into lifeboats, women and children first. Down below, the crew was fighting a losing battle

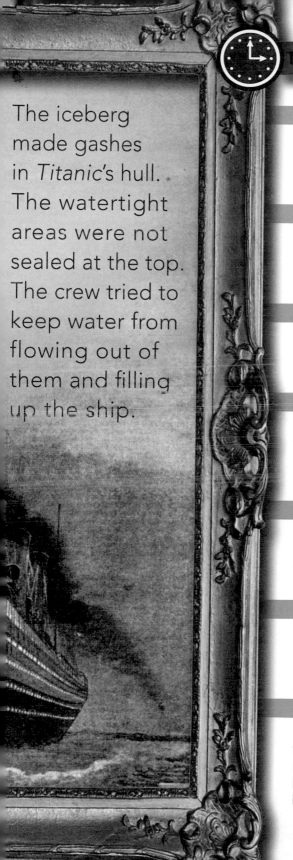

The iceberg made gashes in *Titanic*'s hull. The watertight areas were not sealed at the top. The crew tried to keep water from flowing out of them and filling up the ship.

14 April, 11:40 PM

The iceberg badly damaged *Titanic*'s hull.

14 April, 11:41 PM

The engines went silent. *Titanic* began to drift.

14 April, 11:55 PM

Mail clerks found that their storage room had flooded.

15 April, 12:05 AM

Captain Smith told the crew to get the lifeboats ready.

15 April, 12:15 PM

The band started playing music, to help keep passengers calm.

15 April, 12:25 AM

Thomas Andrews, the ship's designer, knew *Titanic* would sink in two hours.

15 April, 12:25 AM

Titanic radioed for help from any nearby ships: "We have collision with iceberg. Sinking."

Benjamin Hart put his wife and daughter into Lifeboat 14. He watched as it was lowered. But a lot of people felt safer on the ship and would not climb into the lifeboats. Many were launched only half full. Then it became clear that there were not enough lifeboat seats for everyone

SOS

The last two canvas-sided lifeboa

on *Titanic*. At least one officer fired his gun in the air to keep men from storming onto one of the lifeboats. As *Titanic* filled with water, the crew struggled to launch the four canvas-sided lifeboats, like the one in this picture.

***Titanic* life jacket**
Life jackets had cork inside them, to keep wearers afloat.

Eva Hart saw the ship

[My father] said: 'They are going to launch the boats. Purely a precaution; you will all be back on board for breakfast.'

...ere washed into the sea as *Titanic* sank.

The last moments

Horrified survivors watched from the lifeboats as *Titanic*'s rows of glowing lights moved down towards the water. Then the sea flowed over the front of the ship. *Titanic* broke into two parts. Its bow sank straight away. The stern rose up in the air, with people clinging to decks that had become walls. Then it sank, dropping people into the freezing sea. Survivors heard their screams for help, then there was silence.

NEW WORD

The **bow** (bau), or front of a boat, is opposite the **stern** (sturn), or back.

SAY IT OUT LOUD

Should we stay away?

The people in the lifeboats argued. Should they go back for those in the water? Some were afraid that they would all drown if too many people climbed in.

Titanic splits

Titanic split in two, and its bow fell away.

Should we return?

Others felt that they should try to save lives. Officer Harold Lowe moved people to make room. He rowed a lifeboat back and pulled four people from the sea.

Floating stern

The stern floated for a minute. It rose up. Then it plunged to the seabed.

Carpathia picked up all of Titanic's survivors.

Most of Titanic's lifeboats were stored on Carpathia.

Carpathia, another ship, was 93 kilometres (58 miles) from Titanic. It dodged icebergs through the night and found Titanic's lifeboats and their freezing passengers. Many survivors had lost everything except the clothes on their backs. Carpathia's

Carpathia's passengers helped the survivors and gave them clothes to keep them warm.

Survivors' names were radioed ahead to New York.

A large crowd greeted the survivors when they landed.

passengers gave what they could. Most of the survivors were women and children. They searched *Carpathia* for husbands, sons, and brothers. Eva Hart had been parted from her mother when people were moved between lifeboats. She was alone when she was put in a large bag and lifted onto *Carpathia*. Eva knew her father was lost, but she found her mother.

> I started screaming for [my mother]. . . . It was not until we had all been picked up that we found each other, many hours later.

Eva Hart saw the ship

Sea robot

Jason is a deep-sea robot that was used to find *Titanic*.

Discovered!

For 73 years, no one knew where *Titanic* lay. Then, in 1985, a US-French expedition sent a robot down into the ocean and found the stern on the seabed. This showed that *Titanic* had broken into two sections before sinking. The bow was found 600 metres (1,970 ft) away.

Sonar image

This computer-made image shows *Titanic*'s bow on the seabed.

THINK ABOUT IT **Is it right or wrong t**

Bottles of wine

Luggage

A bathtub

More expeditions explored the famous wreck. Thousands of items were taken from the seabed.

Finding *Titanic* sparked interest in the tale of its sinking. Many books and films have told the stories of the heroes and villains on the "ship of dreams". They ask, could things have been different?

Titanic's propeller blades sit on the seabed...

What do you think?

Here are some of the things that went wrong for *Titanic*. Could they have been different? Read your book again. What do you think?

High speed

Titanic sailed towards an ice field at high speed, ignoring radio warnings.

Watertight areas

The tops were not sealed. If one overflowed, the next one flooded.

Lost binoculars

The lookouts could not see very far. Their binoculars were missing.

Bad decision

Captain Smith did not change course to avoid the ice field.

Not enough lifeboats

There were no lifeboats on the first-class deck, because they spoiled the sea view.

No practice

A lifeboat drill was cancelled. The crew had not practised lowering all the lifeboats. They struggled to do it quickly.

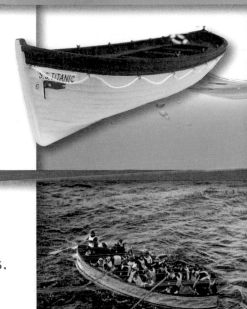

Wasted space

Many lifeboats left with empty seats. Most did not return for survivors.

Californian

Another ship, *Californian*, was only about 27 kilometres (17 miles) away. It did not come to help.

Distress signals

The captain ignored *Titanic*'s distress rockets. He thought they were just greetings.

Glossary

binoculars
A tool that makes distant objects look larger and clearer.

boiler
A device that heats water and produces steam to provide power to something.

bow
The front of a boat or ship.

café
A small restaurant.

canvas
A type of coarse, strong cloth.

cling
To hold on to something very tightly.

collision
A violent coming together of two things.

distress
Danger, or the state of needing help.

drift
To be moved by water or wind, not by a person or an engine.

electricity
A kind of power that travels through wires.

engine
A machine that makes something move.

expedition
A long trip made for a specific reason, such as for exploration.

eyewitness
Someone who saw something happen and can describe it.

gash
A long, deep cut or hole.

hull
The frame or body of a boat or ship.

iceberg
A large piece of ice floating in the sea.

kennel
A place where pets can stay while their owners are away.

Titanic **sank in 2 hours and 40 minutes...**

launch
To move a boat or ship into the water.

lifeboat
A small, strong boat carried on a larger boat and used in emergencies.

life jacket
A jacket that keeps a person afloat.

lights-out
A signal that it is time to turn out the lights and go to sleep.

liner
A large, luxurious ship.

lookout
Someone who keeps watch for danger or trouble.

luxurious
Grand, comfortable, and expensive.

plunge
To fall heavily or sink quickly.

porthole
A small, round window in a boat or ship.

precaution
Something done in advance to keep something dangerous from happening.

promenade
A relaxing walk.

propeller
A set of rotating blades that moves something through air or water.

radio
A device that sends and receives messages, or to send a message using a radio.

rivet
A bolt that holds pieces of metal together.

seabed
The floor of the sea.

shipwreck
The destruction or remains of a ship at sea.

sister ship
A ship that is exactly or almost exactly the same as another ship.

sonar
A method of finding things underwater by using sound waves.

SOS
A distress signal, used by a ship or a plane that needs help.

stern
The back of a boat or ship.

stoker
Someone who keeps a boiler supplied with fuel.

survivor
Someone who lives through a disaster.

swerve
To turn suddenly, to avoid hitting something.

villain
A person who is blamed for something bad that happens.

watertight
Completely sealed so that water cannot get in or out.

Index

Image credits

Photography and artwork

1: World History Archive/Image Asset Management Ltd./Alamy Images; 2tl: yurchyks/iStockphoto; 2–3 (background): National Archives and Records Administration; 2–3 (railing b): Pavel Losevsky/Fotolia; 3bc: ClausAlwinVogel/iStockphoto; 3br: National Archives and Records Administration; 4tl: F. G. O. Stuart/Wikipedia; 4–5 (water background t): danilovi/iStockphoto; 4–5 (gold frame), 4 (photo border, used throughout): subjug/iStockphoto; 4 (photo): AP Images; 4 (round water border, used throughout): iStockphoto/Thinkstock; 4 (cartoon ship, used throughout): akvlv/iStockphoto; 5 (main image): 20th Century Fox/Archive Photos/Getty Images; 6–7 (main image): World History Archive/Image Asset Management Ltd./Alamy Images; 6 (Smith): Wikipedia; 6 (crew): Science Source; 6bl: Miaow Miaow/Wikipedia; 6bc: Paul Fleet/Shutterstock; 6br: Xtuv Photography/Shutterstock; 7bl: DNY59/iStockphoto; 7bcl: t_kimura/iStockphoto; 7bcr: topshotUK/iStockphoto; 7br: Cameramannz/iStockphoto; 8–9 (main image): Popperfoto/Getty Images; 9 (life preserver): ClausAlwinVogel/iStockphoto; 9 (headset): jimd_stock/iStockphoto; 9 (*Titanic* diagram): Tim Loughhead/Precision Illustration; 10–11t: Ralph White/Corbis Images; 10 (map): Planetary Visions Ltd./Science Source; 10–11 (violin, case): Phil Yeomans/BNPS; 11tr: Bain News Service/Library of Congress; 11tc: AP Images; 11tr: Wikipedia; 12–13 (waves background): pixhook/iStockphoto; 12–13 (seabed background): iStockphoto/Thinkstock; 12–13 (main image): Tim Loughhead/Precision Illustration; 13tr: White Star Photo Library; 13cr: Bedford Lemere & Co/National Maritime Museum, Greenwich, London/Royal Museums Greenwich; 13br: Interfoto/Mary Evans Picture Library; 14–15 (background): Kamyshko/iStockphoto; 14bl: Popperfoto/Getty Images; 15t: English School/The Bridgeman Art Library/Getty Images; 15b: Popperfoto/Getty Images; 16–17 (porthole): yurchyks/iStockphoto; 16–17 (main image): pkline/iStockphoto; 17 (side of ship): Eugenesergeev/Dreamstime; 17 (clock): Julie Felton/iStockphoto; 17 (others, t to b):

Mlenny/iStockphoto, Scholastic Inc., DutchScenery/iStockphoto, Bebeto Matthews/AP Images, jimd_stock/iStockphoto, bjeayes/iStockphoto, Scholastic Inc.; 18–19 (large gold frame): subjug/iStockphoto; 18–19 (main image): Universal Images Group/Getty Images; 19 (clock): Julie Felton/iStockphoto; 19 (small frame): gbrundin/iStockphoto; 19 (others, t to b): Mlenny/iStockphoto, World History Archive/Image Asset Management Ltd./Alamy Images, pixhook/iStockphoto, Wikipedia, pixhook/iStockphoto, laurien/iStockphoto, PeterAustin/iStockphoto; 20–21 (main image): National Archives and Records Administration; 21cr: Sang Tan/AP Images; 22–23 (main images): Tim Loughhead/Precision Illustration; 23tr: Wikipedia; 23br: National Archives and Records Administration; 24tl: maritimeques com/Wikipedia; 24tr: Universal Images Group/Getty Images; 24–25b: akg-images; 25tl: Pictorial Press Ltd./Alamy Images; 25tr: Underwood & Underwood/Corbis Images; 26–27 (background t): iStockphoto/Thinkstock; 26tl: Julia DeMarines, Woods Hole Oceanographic Institution/NOAA; 26bl: National Geographic Society/Corbis Images; 27tl, 27tc: Institute for Exploration/Center for Ocean Exploration at the University of Rhode Island/NOAA; 27tr: RMS *Titanic*, Inc./dapd/AP Images; 27br: RMS *Titanic*, Inc./AP Images; 28 (*Titanic* tl): F. G. O. Stuart/Wikipedia; 28 (iceberg): pkline/iStockphoto; 28 (wave): pixhook/iStockphoto; 28 (engine room): Norman Gryspeerdt/ITV Global/The Kobal Collection/Art Resource; 28 (binoculars): Bebeto Matthews/AP Images; 28 (Smith): Wikipedia; 28 (*Titanic* br), 29 (promenade): Popperfoto/Getty Images; 29 (water background): pixhook/iStockphoto; 29 (lifeboat b, *Californian*): National Archives and Records Administration; 29 (firework): Yarygin/iStockphoto; 29 (flare): Brasil2/iStockphoto; 30–31: Tim Loughhead/Precision Illustration; 32: Ralph White/Corbis Images; all others: Scholastic Inc.

Cover
Front cover: (border) Fitzer/iStockphoto; (waves icon) Seamartini/Dreamstime; (main image) Popperfoto/Getty Images. Back cover: (tr) TonyBaggett/iStockphoto; (computer monitor) Manaemedia/Dreamstime. Inside front cover: Scholastic Inc.